Monarchs Migrate

by Melissa Burke

Scott Foresman
is an imprint of

PEARSON

Glenview, Illinois • Boston, Massachusetts • Mesa, Arizona
Shoreview, Minnesota • Upper Saddle River, New Jersey

Photographs
Every effort has been made to secure permission and provide appropriate credit for photographic material. The publisher deeply regrets any omission and pledges to correct errors called to its attention in subsequent editions.

Unless otherwise acknowledged, all photographs are the property of Pearson Education, Inc.

Photo locators denoted as follows: Top (T), Center (C), Bottom (B), Left (L), Right (R), Background (Bkgd).

3 ©Purestock/Alamy; 4 (BL) ©George D. Lepp/Corbis, (BR) ©altrendo nature/Getty Images; 5 (BL) ©Gary Vestal/Getty Images, (BR) Getty Images; 6 ©Karen Tweedy-Holmes/Corbis; 8 ©Frans Lanting/Minden Pictures; 10 (BL) Getty Images, (BR) ©Schafer & Hill /Peter Arnold, Inc.; 11 ©Nigel Marven/Nature Picture Library; 12 (BL) ©Frans Lanting/Minden Pictures, (BR) ©Jeff Foott/Getty Images; 13 ©Catherine Gehm/Getty Images; 15 ©Neo Edmund/Shutterstock

ISBN 13: 978-0-328-39322-0
ISBN 10:   0-328-39322-3

Copyright © Pearson Education, Inc. or its affiliate(s). All Rights Reserved.
Printed in the United States of America. This publication is protected by copyright and permission should be obtained from the publisher prior to any prohibited reproduction, storage in a retrieval system, or transmission in any form or by any means, electronic, mechanical, photocopying, recording, or otherwise. For information regarding permission(s), write to: Pearson School Rights and Permissions, One Lake Street, Upper Saddle River, New Jersey 07458.

Pearson and Scott Foresman are trademarks, in the U.S. and/or other countries, of Pearson Education, Inc. or its affiliate(s).

1 2 3 4 5 6 7 8 9 10 V010 17 16 15 14 13 12 11 10 09 08

Most **insects** can **survive** long cold winters. Monarch butterflies cannot survive cold winters.

What do these butterflies do to survive? They do not **hibernate** like bears. Monarch butterflies **migrate**, or move to another place. They go south to a warmer place.

This is a Monarch butterfly.

Which Monarchs migrate?

All monarchs grow from caterpillars into butterflies. Monarchs that are born in the late summer and early fall will become butterflies as the weather grows cold. These butterflies are special because they will go on a long trip!

How a Monarch Grows and Changes

A Monarch begins as an egg.

The caterpillar eats and grows.

How do the butterflies get ready to migrate?

The Monarchs need a lot of food to get ready for their flight. They store fat to use on their trip. During their trip, they will stop and eat much more food. Without this food and fat, the Monarchs would not be able to get to where they are going.

The caterpillar changes.

The caterpillar becomes a butterfly.

How do Monarchs know it is time to migrate?

Scientists don't know for sure how Monarchs know that it's time to migrate. Cooler **temperatures** may be one clue for the butterflies. Shorter days could be another clue.

Where do Monarchs go?

Where Monarchs go depends on where they start. Some Monarchs fly south, and some Monarchs fly south and west. Many Monarchs go to California, and others fly farther south to Mexico. The trip might be thousands of miles! Monarchs take the longest trip of any butterfly.

This map shows where Monarchs travel.

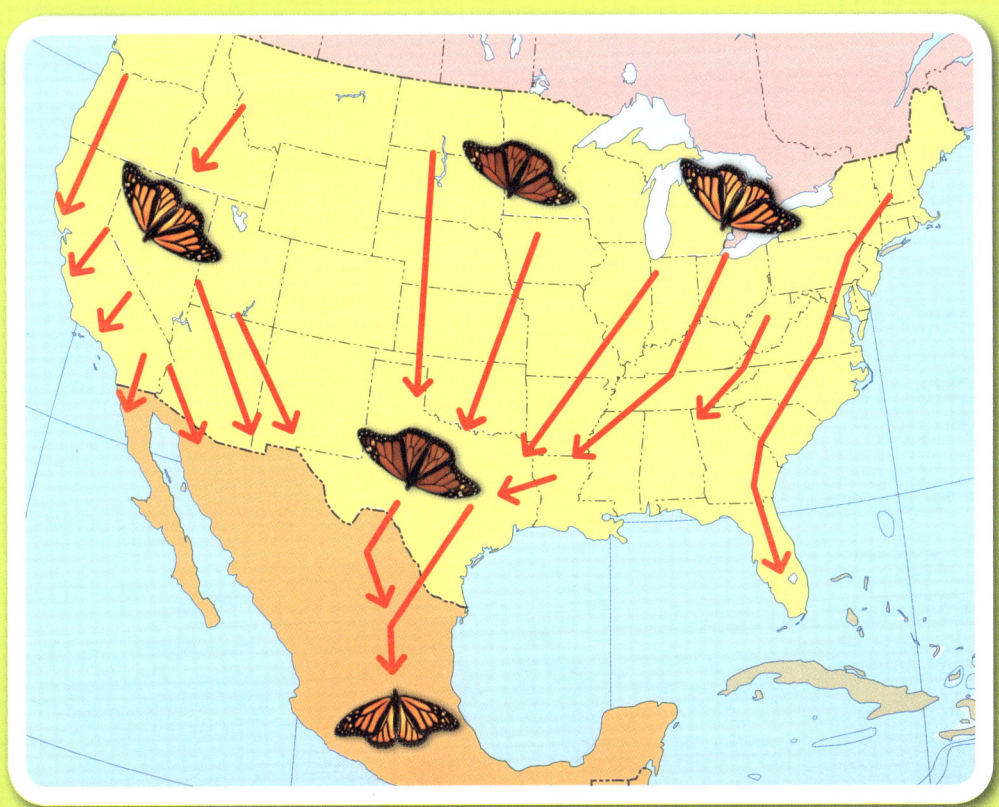

How do Monarchs know where to go?

This is one of the biggest questions! No one knows for sure. The new butterflies have never made this trip before. There is nothing to show them the way. They just know where to go.

Monarchs use the wind to help them fly.

What happens during the trip?

Sometimes monarchs fly in groups. They fly higher or lower because of the wind. They use the wind to help them move along.

Do the butterflies eat and rest?

At times, the butterflies stop to eat. They mostly drink **nectar** from flowers. The monarchs also rest each night. They need rest because the trip can take two months! During the trip, they must dodge enemies. Some birds and other insects eat monarchs.

The Monarch uses nectar for food.

Spiders are one enemy of the Monarch.

What do the Monarchs do all winter?

After their trip, the Monarchs stay in trees in the south. They don't eat much. They move their wings quickly to stay warm.

Wind and rain can blow the butterflies down from the trees. They work to get back with their group. It is safest for them to be close together.

Monarchs stay together to keep warm.

What happens when the butterflies arrive?

In Mexico, the butterflies fly to the top of the mountains. The sky looks like an orange and black cloud because of the butterflies. They land in the trees. They wedge themselves close together to stay warm.